DISCUSSING DIFFICULT TOPICS WITH YOUR KIDS:

Keys on discussing difficult topics with your kids

Julian M. Fields

Table of contents

Chapter 1

Difficult topic: an age-to-age guide

- One of the hardest duties of parenting is talking to your kids about unpleasant themes. It's hard enough to explain when a favorite lovey gets devoured by the washing machine, or when a bully behaves difficult at school. But it might seem hard to put into words some of the very serious concerns, such as war, violence, racism, and other vital themes.

- But in the age of frequent alerts, streaming video, and 24-hour news coverage—when even tiny kids are exposed to truly serious stories—necessary it's to address this problem head-on.

- Addressing the difficult issues helps your kids feel safer, deepens your relationship, and educates them about the world.

- And when you teach children how to obtain and understand information, ask questions, and cross-check sources, they become critical thinkers. It's always hard to tackle the difficulties the world hasn't been able to solve. But by investing our kids with education, compassion, and strong character, we can give them all the skills they need to make things better.

- When your kids hear about something unpleasant or upsetting, most parents experience that deer-in-the-headlights sensation. But it's always a good idea to use your kid's age and developmental stage as a guide to initiating dialogues since they absorb information differently as they grow from newborns to adolescents.

- Understanding a little about how kids see the world in each period of their development helps you communicate knowledge about it in the most age-appropriate manner. Of course, every kid contributes his or her unique sensitivities, temperament, experience, and other distinctive features to every dialogue. So use your best judgment as to how your youngster tends to take in information to choose how deep to go. Here's how you speak to kids aged 2 to adolescent about challenging themes based on childhood-development recommendations.

Age 2 to age 6

Young children don't have enough life experience to comprehend some of the factors involved in complicated, challenging issues. They also don't have a clear grasp of abstract notions or cause and effect. Because they and their key connections (mom, dad, siblings, grandparents, even the family dog) are the centers of their existence, they concentrate on how things influence them.

They're particularly sensitive to parents' emotional moods and often fear that they did something to make you angry. All of this makes it tough to communicate huge topics. On the other side, you're better able to regulate their media exposure, and they can typically move on very soon.

- **Keep the news at bay:** Do everything you can to restrict little kids' exposure to age-inappropriate issues by turning off or muting the TV and selecting material that's geared to their age.

- **Address feelings—yours and theirs. Say, "It's alright to feel terrified, sad, or bewildered:** Those sentiments are normal and we all experience them." Also try: "I'm unhappy, but I'm not upset not with you."

- **Catch your prejudices:** We all have them. Say, "man," "woman," "person," "girl," and "boy," not "big guy," "homeless lady," "beautiful young kid," or "white boy." Avoid discussing a person's race, sexual identity, weight, socioeconomic position, and so on unless it's germane to the topic.

- **Use words, concepts, and connections that they're acquainted with:** Recall a recent, comparable occurrence from their life that they can connect to. Say, "A person stole something. Remember when someone snatched your lunchbox?"

- **Use simple phrases for sensations such as "angry," "sad," "afraid," "glad" and "surprised."** Young toddlers comprehend emotions, but they don't entirely grasp mental illness. You might state that someone was upset too much or puzzled too much and required more support. Avoid idiomatic terms such as "blew a gasket" or "flew the coop."

- **Communicate that someone's in control:** Say, "Mommy and daddy will make sure nothing horrible occurs to our family."

Age 7 to age 12

kids in this age group can read and write, they are exposed to age-inappropriate information more often—but younger kids in this range are still a bit hazy on what's real and fake. As youngsters grow abstract-thinking abilities, real-world experience, and the capacity to articulate themselves, they can wrestle with challenging themes and grasp other views.

- **Wait until the proper time:** At this age, kids are still extremely likely to come to you if they've heard about anything terrible. You may feel them out to determine whether they want to talk about anything, but if they don't bring it up, don't feel you have to address tough things until they ask.
- **Create a safe area for dialogue:** Say, "some things are hard to discuss, even for adults. Let's just chat. I won't be furious, and I want you to feel free to ask whatever you want."

- **Provide background and perspective:** Kids need to grasp the context surrounding a problem to completely make sense of it. For a mass shooting, you may remark, "the individual who committed this had abnormalities in his head that jumbled his thinking." For race-based crimes, try, "some individuals incorrectly feel that light-skinned people are better than dark-skinned people. Without the correct information, they sometimes commit crimes they think are justified."

- **Address their curiosity:** If your youngster stumbles onto grown-up stuff online, it may be time to locate content that will enable them to learn about more adult issues age-appropriately. Say, "internet pornography is something that some grown-ups look at. But it's not about love or romance and it might give you an incorrect notion about sex. If you want to understand more about sex, I can offer you some books to look at and we can chat further if you have questions." Or if your youngster wants to investigate serious themes in more detail than you can supply, say, "let's discover some news sites that provide current events designed for kids. "

- **Be sympathetic to youngsters' emotions and temperament:** You never know what may provoke your youngster. Check in by discussing how you feel and asking them how they feel. Say, "I feel indignant when I realize that someone was wounded." Or, "It makes me feel terrible to learn that someone didn't obtain a proper education or the correct therapy to assist them." And, "what are you experiencing right now?"

- **Encourage critical thinking:** Ask open-ended questions to inspire students to think more thoroughly about critical subjects. Ask, "what did you hear?" "What did it make you think?" and "why do you think that?" For older kids, you may question, "do you think families from various backgrounds would regard this the same way as us?"

- **Look for positives:** There may not be a silver lining to every cloud, but strive to stay positive. Say, "a lot of individuals are behaving like heroes to protect their nation." Or, "let's identify methods that we can aid."

Teens

At this age, adolescents are involved with media freely by reading it, engaging with it, and even generating their own and distributing it in the form of comments, videos, and memes. They frequently hear about challenging things in the news or from other sources, including in video game discussions or on social media, without your knowledge. They're considerably more interested in what their friends or online individuals think about an issue than in your perspective, frequently skipping to the bottom of a post to see user replies before they even read the complete piece. They might bristle at parental lectures because they believe they know better, so encourage them to acquire material that can improve their knowledge and ask questions that urge them to think through their ideas.

- **Encourage open conversation:** Teens need to know that they may ask questions, test their ideas, and talk freely without fear of punishment. Say, "we may not agree on everything, but I'm interested in what you have to say."
- **Ask open-ended questions and ask them to support their ideas:**

Say, "what do you think about police brutality?" "what do you know about it?" "Who do you believe is at fault?" and "why do you think that?"

- **Admit when you don't know anything:** As kids advance into the adolescent era, it's OK for them to recognize that their parents may not have all the answers. Say, "I don't know. Let's attempt to find out more."

- **Get them to ponder the complexity of challenging themes:** Forces like societal challenges, politics, and tradition all contribute to making certain diseases appear incurable. Ask, "what makes difficult issues, such as rape, violence, and crime so hard to solve?" "what key things would need to change to fix certain issues, such as poverty?" "how do policymakers get to the bottom of an issue to correct tough problems?" and "should we accept tiny changes that help a problem little by little or insist on big changes?"

- **Share your values:** Let your kids know where you stand on topics and explain why you hold particular views. If you want your kids to be tolerant of others' differences, for example, explain why you value tolerance and acceptance.

- **Talk about "their" news:** Prompt them to evaluate how various sources put their spin on the problems and how it shapes an audience's perspective of an issue. Facebook, Instagram, and Snapchat tend to bring you material from friends with tales that seem to corroborate one point of view. How do these tales compare to news broadcasts on TV? How about sources created for millennials, like Vice and Vox that have reporters exploring topics in the trenches? Ask, "does a reporter have to experience that circumstance to be able to cover a piece about opiate addiction?"

- **Ask what they would do if they were in a truly tough circumstance:** Teens are discovering their selves and sometimes seek out danger. Considering how they would respond if presented with a horrific reality appeals to their sense of adventure and is a technique to persuade kids to struggle with ethical challenges and imagine themselves making positive choices. Say, "if you were trapped in a political rally that became violent and you watched people being abused, what would you do?"

- **Get them to consider solutions:** Teens might be cynical, but they can also be idealistic. If anything is going to become better, it's this generation who's going to make it happen. Show them that you trust them for the job. Ask, "If you were in charge, what issue would you solve first—and how would you do it?"

Chapter 2

Share your feelings with your kids

Set aside time every day to discuss together and exchange thoughts about the day. If feasible, allocate a set time (for example, shortly before sleep or after a meal) to reflect on and chat about the day.

Make your house a secure atmosphere where your children feel comfortable expressing their ideas, emotions, anxieties, and frustrations without criticism. By establishing a setting where sharing and listening may take place freely, you are conveying a message that their ideas and emotions are important and you are helping to model appropriate methods to cope with them.

You are the expert on your kid. By looking at the "big picture" of their growth and development at school and home, you may assist identify their strengths and areas for support. Share your child's hobbies and learning style with your child's instructor.

When your kid is experiencing a challenging time, it might be useful for them to take a little pause to calm down, recharge, or concentrate. This might include getting up to grab a sip of water, sitting quietly for a few minutes, and/or completing a calming stretch or deep breathing exercise. Practicing coping skills like these with you in calmer circumstances helps your kid learn how to cope with powerful emotions and challenging difficulties on their own.

When children understand and regulate their emotions properly, they become more confident and eager to take on new tasks at home and school. Encourage your children to share their ideas and emotions with you. If it is hard for them to speak about their emotions, advise them to try writing it in a notebook or drawing a picture about their day or an event they had.

Sometimes deeds speak louder than words. Make conscious decisions to put your gadgets down and eliminate distractions to participate in concentrated one-on-one time

with your kid. Giving them your entire attention and doing something pleasant together tells them that you care about their happiness and well-being and that you value spending time together
Find out what they know

Chapter 3

Tell your kids the truth

It is very amazing to witness the contrast between adults and children when it comes to stating the truth. Adults are typically eager to conceal things, particularly if they appear unpleasant or painful. Kids, on the other hand, are often honest to a fault (and sometimes to the disgust of their parents!) and talk freely about their thoughts and ideas. What's intriguing, then, is the habit of sheltering children from the reality. Not only is it a formula for mistrust, but also harmful on multiple levels.

Reasons

- **They should hear it from someone they trust:** Wouldn't it be lovely if life didn't ever suck? If life was predictable and mild, and we never had to worry about pain or unpleasantness? But that's simply not the case. Life occurs and sometimes it happens to hurt. We think that, where feasible, children should be exposed to the ups and downs from the people they trust most. By talking about the tough stuff at home first, it helps to normalize difficult topics and create an atmosphere of honesty. If we are honest with our kids, they feel like they can be more honest with us.

- **Resilience starts at home**: Helicopter Parenting (or the new appropriately titled Lawnmower Parenting) might be seductive. Of course we want to safeguard our children. Of course we want to fight their fights for them. Of course we don't want children to feel sad or uncomfortable. Our responses are natural and it's hard not to yield into them. But we need to assist our young to acquire the abilities they need to cope with things like rejection and disappointment. They can construct those support tools in a thousand tiny ways and honest, judgment -free talks are vital.

- **We can assist children develop empathy for others**: Some individuals are inherently incredibly empathic whereas it doesn't seem to come readily to others. We can't expect tiny children to sympathize on a profound level with individuals who are hurting and yet frequently they do. Perhaps they're smart souls or perhaps they're inherently more honest. The more we can explain the sentiments and emotions underlying life experiences, the more children may develop empathy and even resilience. If we can encourage their natural propensity to be honest, we can help develop strong roots that will nourish them as they grow.

- **Honesty is the key to more wonderful things**: Being honest is a vital life skill that can make a world of difference. It opposes ignorance and entitlement and fosters learning and attention. We everyone should ask more questions, acknowledge when we don't know the answer and be more open-minded. It's remarkable how when someone won't confess they don't know anything, they also won't admit they're sorry and they won't accept there's anything wrong with it. Honesty makes us more open, inquiring and welcoming.

- **They will establish a deeper trust with you:**The more we inform our kids and trust them with the truth, the more we develop an honest discourse. It doesn't mean we need to go home and tell our kids how Susan from work was pissing us off today. It simply means delivering honest answers invites more honest queries. More often than not, the uncomfortable person in the room isn't the youngster but the adult. The question is why are we uncomfortable? Perhaps it's because we don't know where to start or have the correct words. A smart strategy is to go with your intuition, be as honest as you believe is acceptable and comprehensible for your youngster. And when in doubt, discover the tools you need to start communicating.

Avoiding the questions or painful lessons doesn't mean they go away, it simply means our kids will stop turning to us for the solutions.So don't worry if the response isn't great.
Just keep chatting.

Chapter 4

Reassure your kids

For many youngsters, your presence will help soothe them. Hug them or hold them on your lap. Even holding their hand might help offer them a feeling of security and comfort.

Having the ability to communicate what you're feeling is vital, particularly for youngsters. Give them some one-on-one time and listen without criticizing or dismissing their concern. The greatest time to speak things out is when they are feeling calm since they can listen to you more readily. Telling your youngster that "everything will be okay," could instead reinforce to your child that there is reason to worry. While it's hard to resist the impulse to comfort your youngster that everything will be well, it could be beneficial in the long run.

If your kid has problems talking about why they are frightened, there are various ways to start the dialogue. Ask them to create a picture or play out what they are scared of using a doll, puppet, or stuffed animal.

Not knowing how to assist may be challenging and upsetting for parents, but don't let those feelings show. Your youngster can sense how you're feeling. Revealing your feelings might make your kid feel like they've offended you, raise their anxiousness, and make talking more difficult. Try to provide an example of how to respond quietly to assist your youngster to feel calmer, as well. Even if what they are scared of seems foolish to you, it's vital to show your kid that you understand. Although they may not genuinely have something to be scared of, the feelings they are experiencing are quite real.